MW00329880

The Wounded Leader

*The True Identity of the Superhero
Revealed through the Eyes
of His Alter Ego*

Shaun Saunders

Shaun Saunders
Jonesboro, Georgia

Cover design by TLH Designs, Chicago, IL
www.tlhdesigns.com

Book design by Kingdom Living Publishing, Fort Washington, MD www.kingdomlivingbooks.com

For information about this book or to contact the author, write to:

Pastor Shaun Saunders
100 North Creek Trail
Jonesboro, GA 30238

You may also send the author an email message at
thewoundedleader12@gmail.com

Published by:
Shaun Saunders
Jonesboro, GA

Published in the United States of America.

ISBN 978-0-615-65497-3

Dedication

To the millions of people around the world who have failed to live up to the unrealistic expectations of the flawless superhero your followers require and call for you to be, may this book encourage you to reveal the true identity of your wounded leader hiding behind the shadow of the superhero you aspire to be.

To the late Estella Ada Beasley, the absence of your presence will forever remind me of what a pleasure it was to be your grandson. The moments we were privileged to share with one another throughout the years have allowed me to capture a still image of your beauty. Grandma, I miss you and I will always love you. As I sit, in tears, I promise that your life and legacy will continue to live on through me and my family. I therefore joyfully dedicate this, my first of many books, to you, Estella Ada Beasley, the best grandma I could ever ask for.

To Barbara and John Saunders, my parents, I dedicate this book to you. I applaud you for always affirming, protecting, and preparing me for such a time as this. Despite all the ups and downs we have been through as a family, it has been an honor for me to call you my parents. I love both of you so very much and no matter what you do, my love will never change. Mom and Dad, allow this book to express to the world the wonderful parents you are. I love you.

To my brothers and sisters, I hope this book inspires you to pursue after God's will for your life. The world is waiting for the anointing residing on the inside of you to stand up, so that the God in you can be heard.

To Minister Duane and Val Wallace, thank you for setting an example of what true Christianity is. Minister Wallace you and Aunt Val are the epitome of what every Christian couple should aspire to be. Aunt Val, even though you are no longer here physically, the power of your words and your presence will forever live on in me. I miss you Aunt Val, and I love you Minister Wallace, or Dad. If it were not for you tightening me up and keeping me on the right road, I know this book would have never happened. So to the Wallace family: Min. Dwane, Aunt Val, Morgan, DJ, and Taylor, I dedicate this book to you because you all mean so much to me.

Finally, to every woman patiently waiting for the man God anointed you with the strength to love to evolve into the Boaz he has the potential to become just as God promised you in the Genesis of your relationship, I dedicate this book to you, the only woman equipped with the resources to love him the right way.

Acknowledgments

In May of 2010, I was commissioned by God and endowed with the wisdom of the Holy Spirit to write my first book entitled, "The Wounded Leader." This book took me a little more than one year to write; and there were many people to encourage me throughout the process of its production. The energy, time, and effort I exhausted in order to complete this book would have been to no avail without the support and encouragement of my family, friends, pastors, and co-workers. This book, in my opinion, is a masterpiece, revealing through its content, the countless wounds of leaders whose experiences, pains, tears, and testimonies have exposed me to the knowledge I have revealed in these pages. It is therefore with great honor that I acknowledge the following individuals for assisting me with the completion of this book.

I first would like to thank my beautiful wife Melody and our children, Jeremiah, Sarah, David, and Rachel, for always believing in me and encouraging me to never give up throughout this long and tedious process.

You all truly inspired me to see this project to the end. I love you all so very much.

To Kingdom Living Publishing, I thank you for providing me with a wonderful platform to advertise and market this book. Your services are exceptional and you helped me to make my dream a reality. Thank you so much! I promise that after this book is published you will be happy with its success.

To Carlen and Tamyia Ross, thank you for your friendship and your love. You both have been a blessing to my wife and me, allowing us to revisit, through your relationship, the beauty of when we first fell in love. Through my observance of your coming together to become one, I have gathered some much needed information to plant in the pages of this book. Thank you guys. I love you.

To all the members and staff at the Word of Life Church, thank you for blessing me with the opportunity to be your pastor. You are the reason I refused to give up. May this book inspire you to live life to the fullest.

Table of Contents

Foreword

There are many leaders in the Christian community today who are struggling with living up to their potential while staying grounded in the truth. *The Wounded Leader* challenges us, all of us from the megachurch leader to the storefront pastor, to look in the mirror and get a proper assessment of who we are and whom we serve. Pastor Saunders has done a masterful job of identifying the "alter egos" of leaders, exposing the vulnerabilities and strengths in a way that humanizes us all.

The statement made in the final chapter sums it all up quite effectively: "Jesus' purpose for coming to earth was never to show us God's glory working in Him, but to model an example of God's glory working in us." The glory of God is revealed in all of His leaders from the least to the greatest and this book helps us to keep that fact in focus. Because all of us have been wounded in battle and are therefore Wounded Leaders!

Minister Duane J. Wallace
Associate Minister
Alpha Baptist Church
Willingboro, NJ

Introduction

As creation searches for a way to reconnect with its maker, the earth cries out, longing for the re-emergence of a God fearing leader. A leader, by definition, is one endowed with a special gift and or ability to lead others. The expectation for the one once epitomized as hero gradually fades away from the safety of those places that use to highlight the morals and values of a stable society. The absence of the leader's presence in the home, church, school, politics, and the business world has caused many to expunge the possibility of his existence from their memory. As time continues to pass by, the God fearing image of the leader is radically redefined by a world that demands its leaders to live up to the kind of perfection that exists only in a fantasy world.

In the heart of every leader the desire to live up to the superficial expectations of a fictitious superhero has deceived many into prostituting their gift to the faltering imagination of an audience never satisfied with his efforts. Now instead of restoring the presence of an image that reveals the intent of God's original idea, the leader appeals more to the fame of the super-hero, while underestimating the valued presence of his wounded personality. A leader's inability to confront the gruesome reality of his secret identity further distorts the perception of the God image every leader was created to reflect. As a result, many have chosen to run away from their failures, hoping to escape the shameful activity of the unruly individual they have denied the right to exist.

After years of dodging to elude the scars of unhealed wounds, the voice of the leader's usually silent personality declares his independence from the perfections of a fantasy that refuses to acknowledge his existence. Confronted with the announcement of his alter ego, the superhero is examined thoroughly under the auspices of his neglected partner to measure the integrity of his public life and to expose the man he forgot to mention to others he is behind close door. The legacy of a God fearing leader can only be appreciated through the confession of his weakness, exemplifying the true source of his strength. The true source of every leader's strength is located in the life of Jesus Christ. Evidence of Jesus' power to heal, liberate, and deliver are no longer submitted as verifiable proofs to confirm the working of His power in humanity, because of the unwillingness of those who lead to be transparent.

The success of the superhero can only be measured by the testimony of the freak that came out, or possibly still comes out in the dark hours of a leader's life. In order for the leader's intended audience to celebrate the tremendous heights he has successfully climbed, they must at some point be exposed to the deep depths God had to reach down to rescue him from the pains of his wounds. This is the testimony of every leader afflicted with the severe pains of wounds that still bleed. This is voice of the one looking for anyone to revive his soul. This is the cry of the Wounded Leader, a superhero revealed through the eyes of his alter ego.

Chapter One

Let's Get Ready to Rumble

The silent cries and blood gushing wounds of those called, elected, and appointed to lead echo the sounds of the contaminated soul, infected by the failure of the afflicted to apply the ointments and proper bandages necessary to heal their open wounds. Now numb to the pain from which they once longed and desired to be healed, the reality of the indestructible force everyone expects leaders to be begins to slowly fade away into the darkness of those wounds that cause their body's dis-ease. The war between the image and the package, the package through which the image is revealed, challenges those who lead to closely examine and find a balance between the individuals they are in the light and the dark canvassing of the individuals they are when wounded.

It is important to remember that light, in order for the natural eye to comprehend its existence, can only be revealed through the depths of darkness from which it desires to distinguish itself. The two, however seem to depend on one another, validating each other's need to coexist. Like a husband and wife, light and darkness are united together in holy matrimony. As they unite, fusing together to become one, the product they create through the intimacy they once shared becomes the epitome of an idea both were created to define. The product, or the leader, is the substance of the idea, whose purpose and true identity can only be perceived through the scar he has endured, helping to confirm the integrity and authority behind the idea he was created to represent. The depth of a leader's effectiveness is measured by the degrees of compassion he extends on those individuals under his leadership. Within the context of Scripture the writer of the book of Hebrews shares with us in Chapter Five verses one and two that,

> *Every High Priest taken from among men is ordained for men in things pertaining to God, that he may offer for both gifts and sacrifices of sin: Who can have compassion on the ignorant, and on them that are out of the way; for that he himself also is compassed with infirmity* (Hebrews 5:1-2).

The infirmity, or weakness, that besets the priest referred to in verse two is the back drop of darkness that allows light to shine brightly in the eyes of those assigned specifically to the anointing or endowment that flows through the leader. It is here that the leader discovers those wounds that still cry for relief from the lowly place of secrecy, where they were conceived. He now sees how they are esteemed as the fertile ground through which the supernatural power of the hero takes on a tangible form, substantiating the essence of God's power in his present reality. As the fame connected to the power begins to assert itself by addressing the immediate need of the people, the leader's quest after greatness is hindered by the wounds he tries to disguise and cover up, while trying to protect the identity of the hero the people call for him to be.

Like a good painter, leaders sometime feel the need to create an image in the minds of their audience, introducing themselves as a superhero, while failing to acknowledge the wounds associated with the package that looks like the person they are more likely to associate with their conflicting past. So, finally the stage is set and the two sides that once stood together united as one are now facing the possibility of a long and bitter divorce. Can the two, however, exist separate and apart from one another? Is it even possible for the superhero to be the valiant warrior he portrays himself to be without the disguise of the fragilely framed physique of the individual he tries to convince himself he isn't? These are the same questions that leaders must ask themselves. Many of those who have been called to lead must always remember that a great leader has the most profound influence on the people with whom he is willing to be the most transparent. The superhero image leaders have tried to paint in the imagination of those people God has assigned to their vision will forever remain an incomplete masterpiece if they fail to address the wounds of the fallen soldier they are prior to and during their metamorphosis. Leaders must expose the origin of their strength as it is seen through the eyes of the wounded soldier to whom they have denied their dependents access. Leaders ought never to allow the fear of what people think stop them from getting the treatment they need to heal the pains of their untreated wounds. Their enemy is not the people they serve but the quarrel between the two very distinct personalities warring on the inside of them.

As we begin to investigate and examine the wisdom revealed through the pages of this book, I stand as the ring side announcer, preparing you for the fight of your life.

In the one corner, fighting in the bloody trunks, all the way from the land of the wounded,

LADIES AND GENTLEMEN!!!!

Please welcome the CHALLENGER,

the WOUNDED LEADER!!!!

His opponent, fighting in the white trunks with red trim, considers himself to be a gift to the body of believers, an instrument used unto the glory of his God. His critics would say he pretends to be the idea of the man God wishes every woman would desire their husband to be like. He is more honorably recognized as a man after God's heart.

LADIES AND GENTLEMEN!!!!

Please give it up for the sometimes arrogant and self-centered hero,

the CHAMPION, the SUPERHERO!!!!

So now, to all my ladies and gentlemen and to all the wounded leaders around the world:

"LET'S GET READY TO RUMBLE!!!!"

Chapter Two

The Superhero versus the Accusations of His Alter Ego

As the war between the forces of good and evil and light and darkness contend with one another, hoping to conquer the soul of those passionately devoted to their craft, the duel between the two conflicting personalities battling within the mind of the leader take center stage. Both are ready to distance themselves from the inferiority of their opponent. Because of the call to live up to expectations, similar to those placed on a number one pick in the NBA draft, most leaders seem to commit very easily to the flaunting of their gift, while sometimes failing to maintain the same integrity necessary for a successful life outside of the arena where thousands of jovial fans come to appreciate their talents. Understand that within the psyche of everyone chosen either by God or appointed by the people to lead, there is a strong desire for the glory of

Dr. Jekyll, always accommodated unfortunately by the secret life of Mr. Hyde. The reality of this statement has proven to be true, not only in times past but especially in the perverse societies leaders are expected to police today. From the miraculous victories of a shepherd boy named David, who destroyed Goliath, then killed Uriah to cover up his adulterous affair with his wife, to a host of some of today's very well known politicians, athletes, movie stars, and even televangelists, leaders have failed to live up to the expectations of the souls their services were intended to reach out to. In the book of Romans, we are reminded by Paul of the continual struggle between the two natures warring against one another in the mind of the believer:

> *I know that nothing good lives in me, that is, in my sinful nature. For I have a desire to do what is good, but I cannot carry it out. For what I do not want to do—this I keep on doing. Now if I do what I do not want to do, it is no longer I who do it, but it is sin living in me that does it. So I find this law at work: When I want to do good, evil is always right there with me. For in my inner being I delight in God's law; but I see another law at work in the members of my body, waging war against the law of my mind and making me a prisoner of the law of sin at work within my members* (Romans 7:18-23, NIV).

Yes! Finally an example of a leader willing to expose the loads of dirty laundry under the tough, macho man, superhero exterior so many of them like to portray themselves off as in the eyes of others. Paul's dilemma warns of an inevitable reality all leaders will be confronted with eventually. Though the two natures at war have contrasting motives or purposes, the conflict continues to build up over who has inherited the right to influence the individual space where both are currently cohabitating. The time and space these two natures are striving to occupy is always prepared and ready to accommodate the good that agrees and the bad that conflicts with the original purpose for which it was created and continues to exist. The desire of each side to influence the territory, both synonymously occupy, creates a platform for the two to provide a significant amount of evidence that supports their right to exercise power in the area they claim. The territory referred to in this case is the space within the individual's heart where these two war for total authority. This ultimately makes the individual, through which this tension occurs, the jury that will decide the fate of the two personalities involved in this never ending dual.

The jury will have to render verdicts for each side, declaring one the right to lead, while the other is sentenced to a life time of service to the greater. In Genesis 25:22-23, the theme of dualism spoken of throughout the first few paragraphs in this chapter takes on a tangible form within this context:

The babies jolted each other within her, and she said, "Why is this happening to me?" So she went to inquire of the Lord. The Lord said to her, "Two nations are in your womb and two people from within you will be separated; one people will be stronger than the other, and the older will serve the younger" (Genesis 25:22-23, NIV).

While being formed in the womb of Rebekah, both Jacob and Esau began to wage war on one another over who had a right to the inheritance of the father, bestowed only upon the first born. Through further study of Genesis Chapter 25, we find out that though Esau is the oldest, he relinquished his right to lead by trading in his birthright for a bowl of stew to his younger sibling, Jacob. As their father Isaac began to grow old and his eyes weakened, he was summoned to render his verdict as to the fate of his two sons. Through the deception of their mother, who decided to declare Jacob the right to lead and Esau the lifetime sentence of service, Isaac blessed the younger of his two sons above the eldest. Now even though Isaac, the patriarch, is considered to be the primary decision maker in this story, it is clear that Rebekah believed the reality of God's Word previously spoken to her stating the older will serve the younger. The two brothers as a result, though at odds with one another, would eventually reconcile their relationship.

The question therefore then arises: How can two personalities with conflicting purposes coexist in harmony with one another? The answer to this question can be very simply stated, but is usually difficult to understand. The two natures or personalities that I am referring to are the spirit and the flesh. The extent of the power attached to both personalities is immeasurable. The spirit, however, is more powerful and carries with it an anointing or endowment for the body it has been assigned. The flesh personality tries to hinder the influence of this anointing on the body, which causes the spirit to further reveal its supernatural ability to prevail as the victor over the flesh.

The opposition of the flesh causes those wounded by its ambush to place a greater demand on an anointing that can only reveal itself in places where it is appreciated and needed. The existence of this anointing is realized under the umbrella of imperfect conditions that place a demand on its supernatural power. Through conditions it did not create, but that were created through the desires of the flesh, the existence of the spirit will only be requested and can only be understood through the conflicting forces of flesh that cause it to violently engage its power. So then it is clear one cannot substantiate the tangible reality of the spirit nature without first acknowledging the opposing and contrary nature of the flesh. Likewise, one cannot perceive the reality of the flesh, without being confronted by the internal desire of the spirit nature that wars for the body to be restored back to the original condition for which it was created. It appears then that the two are inseparable. They are two different sides represented on the same coin.

Under the impenetrable armor of many superheroes, there lies the fragilely framed physique of the forgotten individual who lives in the shadow of the hero the people call for him to be. Yes, thank God for Spiderman, but what about Peter Parker. We look forward to the rage of the Incredible Hulk, failing to make the right connection with his angry counterpart, David Banner. How can anyone forget about the caped crusader Batman and his undercover accomplice Bruce Wayne? Or, how can anybody forget the man of steel, Superman, and his decoy, Clark Kent? All of these comic book characters in some way or another have attracted those desiring to lead to the hero's fame without any regard for the hero's pain.

In order to appreciate the accomplishments of the superhero, one must seek to understand the development of the hero from birth to maturity. The Bible says in Galatians 4:12, *"That as long as the heir is a child, he is no different from a slave, although he owns the whole estate. He is subject to guardians and trustees until the time set by his father."* The significance of a father's presence or absences throughout the maturity of a superhero's saga is vitally important when assessing the development of the superhero. During the early stages of his development, his father should have affirmed, inspired, and become the primary source of his understanding. The echoing voice of a father affirms for a young child the undeniable reality of what his heart desires for him to be. His father's voice inspires him to pursue passionately after the mastermind that came up with the idea through which his desire originated.

What! Superheroes have desires? Yes, every superhero desires to be loved and appreciated, not only for his strength, but also in his weakness. As you will see in chapter four of this book, our superhero's desires are uncovered during his emotional love affair and infatuation with the beautiful and vivacious Ms. Destiny. His desire for companionship reveals the loud cries of his wounds, calling out for someone to look through the superhero suite and capture the essences of the lonely and often misunderstood frail person behind the red cape. No matter how long leaders try to run or fly around with their capes on, eventually they will desire for someone to tell them it is okay for them to take them off and enjoy being normal. This component of leadership is called intimacy. Intimacy is the place of secrecy, a hiding place for both the superhero everyone expects them to be and the fragilely framed physique of the forgotten individual they are behind the cape. It is in this place that these two different personalities stand naked and unashamed as they are viewed through the eyes of the one they were created to serve. Most leaders would like for that one lady in their life, through their own personal observation, to at least make the connection that both the hero in them and their silenced alter ego are the same person. It is, however, unfortunate that the blinding light of the hero does not make it easy for their wives and others to make the connection that these two are really one.

Through intimacy leaders cry for those whose eyes are anointed to see, to see them fully in the capacity in which God created them, and not to expect them to be anything more or less than what God said they should be. Most often this never really happens. It is rare for leaders in this lifetime to find at least one pair of eyes that can connect with the issues of their heart outside of the fame that follows them when they put on their superhero costumes. Spiderman, the Hulk, Batman, and yes in my opinion the mack daddy of them all, Mr. Superman, all sought out the opportunity to take off their perfected armor, eager to expose their nakedness and emotional distress, crying and screaming out loudly for some to look In-To-Me-and-See. This is the cry of every leader that for most of them is never heard. This is a clarion call to those very limited number of individuals, maybe one or two, that are able to see them the way God sees them, even when they do not look like what God said they should be. In 1 Samuel 16:7, after Samuel believes God has selected Jessie's son Eliab to be the next King, God shows Samuel how to see the heart of a leader:

> *Do not consider his appearance or his height, for I have rejected him. The Lord does not look at the things man looks at. Man looks at the outward appearance, but the Lord looks at the heart* (1 Samuel 16:7, NIV).

There is no greater intimacy than the intimacy we find while spending time in the presence of our Lord. Our desire for intimacy with another individual is not possible until we first learn how to be intimate with God. Think about it. Is there any one thing about us that we can share with God that He does not already know? He knows everything about us. The Bible speaks about this intimacy in Psalm 139:

> *For you created my inmost being; you knit me together in my mother's womb. I praise you because I am fearfully and wonderfully made: your works are wonderful, I know that full well. My frame was not hidden from you when I was made in the secret place. When I was woven together in the depths of the earth, your eyes saw my unformed body. All the days ordained for me were written in your book before one of them came to be* (Psalm 139:13-15, NIV).

God's ability to look past leaders' protective shields and see into the secret cave they run to, embracing the nakedness of which they once were ashamed, helps them to appreciate the complexity of the package through which the image is revealed. In other words, the degree to which a leader is willing to be honest with God privately will ultimately determine the authenticity of the image he projects publically. His honesty with God helps him to assess his willingness to be totally honest with himself. An as I stated earlier, a great leader has the most profound influence on the people with whom he is willing to be the most transparent.

Because of the leaders unwillingness to be honest with themselves, many of them have failed in their desire to be transparent first with God, second with their wives, and then with those whom they lead. By doing this, they have created in the imaginations of those around them a fantasy starring a flawless superhero, perfect in all his ways, capable of living up to the unrealistic expectations that can only be achieved in a perfect world.

A superhero's decision to hide behind the disguise of the fragilely framed alter ego, the person he is privately, hinders the ability of others to make an intimate connection with him the same way they do with the perfect image of the hero he promises to be. The focus here, however, at this point now begins to shift in the favor of the package. Yes! What about the package? It is just as important, if not more important, to the whole than the image it projects. To be clear, allow me to explain the relationship between the image and the package.

The image is the expression God gives of Himself through us, enabling us and those around us to comprehend His existence within the realm of our immediate reality. The God we serve is an invisible God, who uses the earth's elements to fuse in our imaginations the depths of His unconditional love, strengthening us to carry the weight that accompanies His glory. The heaviness of His presence is then placed within a package that He designed, decorated, wrapped, and set in an environment that can appreciate the gift on the inside, while still infatuated with the beauty of the package through which it was delivered. The package then is the forgotten beauty of the fragilely framed physique God uses to reveal Himself to the world. When leaders are willing to be transparent with others, both the image and the package balance each other out. This balance is necessary because it allows those watching a leader the opportunity to see the beauty these two create when united together in holy matrimony.

Every superhero is the light in the marriage empowering those in trouble with the solutions they need to live an abundant and prosperous life. His alter ego is the backdrop of darkness that allows the light of the man in the costume to be recognized in the mind of those searching for a hero. So when the question arises of whether or not it is possible for a superhero to exist without the disguise of the alter ego, the answer to this question is simply 'no,' because the two have been inseparably fused together to make one.

Our ability to accurately perceive and interpret the oneness that the superhero and his alter ego have come to share can sometimes cause us to confuse the individual responsibilities of each personality represented. As I sat on July 8, 2010, eagerly anticipating the long awaited announcement from the supposed king with no ring, LeBron James, about where he plans to spend the next six years of his career, I realized that some had called into question the celebrity of King James the player and the loyalty of LeBron James the person. It is obvious that by the time this book was released, the King had long made his decision, and was trying to win his first title. What intrigued me the most about this highly publicized announcement was really about how the city of Cleveland responded to their once beloved King after he decided to leave the place where he had promised his loyalty. Even though King James and LeBron James are the same person, the two must always stay in the lane of responsibility each one is expected to live up to. Like Superman, King James is a brand name.

The brand name is a name that generates the fame of the hero by way of an anointing that is revealed through a specific gift or talent. LeBron James, like the alter ego is the package that helps to advertise the product. He is the little boy who grew up in Akron, Ohio, raised by his mother in a single parent home. He is a son and a father who loves his family and desires nothing more than to make sure they are well taken care of. Although the King and his forgotten co-worker LeBron James are two different sides of the same coin, this side of Cleveland's superhero is often overlooked. On July 8 at 9:31 p.m., the once loved, celebrated, and highly respected Cleveland-born hero decided to leave his hometown team and take his talents elsewhere, making him one of the most, if not the most, despised superstars ever in Cleveland sports history. From the fans that once declared their love for him now burning his jersey to his former owner who was ready to invest over 100 million dollars on the superstar now suggesting he is cursed and will never succeed with his new team, the shifting of the supposed appreciation of the hero to the now bitter hatred towards him makes me wonder, "Where is the love?" There really is a thin line between love and hate.

Most often, the love lost for a hero comes from those who loved only his outfit, connecting with him because of what he does and not because of who he is. Their inability and disregard for the personal choices that are made by the man behind the mirror, a reflection they really never desired to know, now darkens their perception of the hero they once devoted their love to. The kind of love that is seen here is motivated by conditions and expectations that call for leaders to be what others want them to be, and not what they need to be for others. By this leaders do a disservice to those to whom their gifts are specifically assigned.

Their ability to discern between what people need and want from them is the standard they must use to measure the extended depths to which they are willing to go in order to comply with the people's demands. In their arrogant attempt to be everyone's everything, leaders yield themselves to the enticing words of their fans, yes their fans crying, "Savior, Savior here my humble cry!" Under the pressure of these high expectations that they have allowed to be placed on them, they crumble and fall, because like the people they serve they cover up their wounds hoping to rid themselves from the guilt they think disqualifies them from being the leader so many look for them to be. A leader has never been and should never be looked at as a savior. Just ask LeBron James. Look at how quickly the Cleveland fans moved on from crying "Savior," to "Kill him." The hope of so many wrapped in a king's declaration of victory was now daunted by the distance between the image they idolized and the person they thought they knew living behind the crown.

This is the personality of the hero leaders wish people could see, accept, and appreciate as they continue to love them despite the tantrums they throw to express the unbearable pain of their wounds. When a leader steps into a room full of people he knows, or does not know, he should always show two forms of identification to prove his right by law to operate in those offices he occupies. Leaders lead not because of their great power, but because of their willingness to share with others their pain. It is only when they are ready to honestly identify the badly scarred body that reminds them of their wounded past and the image that is a reflection of what God expects them to be that they like the prodigal son can honestly say that they have come face to face with themselves. Their failure to acknowledge, or their blatant attempts to deny the very existences of the wounds that have left them scarred, memorials of their pain, gives those amazed by the grace of their superpowers the right to ask a very interesting question, "What happened to the forgotten image of the man in the mirror?"

Chapter Three

The Man in the Mirror

"Man in the Mirror" is a powerful hit song written in the early 90's by the King of Pop, Michael Jackson, one of the most idolized and most misunderstood entertainers of all times. From hit songs like *"Human Nature"* and *"Thriller"* to more controversial songs like *"Black or White,"* Michael Jackson sold out stadiums worldwide filled with fans screaming his name, crying and sweating profusely—all excited about the opportunity to connect with the image of the flawless entertainer. His highly acclaimed hit songs and dance routines caused audiences to stand in awe, totally captivated by his unique style and musical talents. This gave him the perfect getaway to escape from the faltering reflection of the man he failed to confront when he looked in the mirror. As a troubled grown man carelessly attempting to bandage the wounds of the abuse he suffered

early in his childhood, he publicly reflected the life of Dr. Jekyll while privately living the life of Mr. Hyde. Many of his so-called fans fell in love with what he did and how he made them feel, *"The way you make me feel,"* but many of them never learned how to love the scared, angry, frustrated, and lonely little Michael, the fading reflection of the man staring back at him when he looked into the mirror. Like Michael, the reflection of the image we see when we look into the mirror depends largely on the transparency/honesty of the mirror we choose to look into.

The mirror, any of the various reflecting surfaces, is the apparatus leaders look into eager to discover whether or not the person staring back at them is really the person God created and said they should be. So, when you look into the mirror, what does the man staring back at you look like? How does he make you feel? What does he have to say about you?

If leaders were to be brutally honest with themselves, many of them because of their shame, guilt, and regret run far, far away from their reflection hoping to erase it from their memory. Instead of facing their giant, they run and expel his identification from their thoughts, denying his existence in their very real and present reality. They dismiss the package, the dark canvassing of the wounded individuals they are, denying themselves full access to the depths of their Creator's thoughts and intentions toward them. Like a rebellious child longing for the attention of the father that abandoned him, the reflection that the leader has neglected now violently desires to confront the authenticity of the flawless hero that fails to acknowledge his existence.

Through years of dishonesty and playing hide and go seek with the reflection he despises and hates, the flawless hero that once believed he was invincible is now forced to answer his neglected foe when he is asked, "How could you forget about me?" Now afraid, standing face to face with the wounded reflection he thought he had successfully eluded for so many years, the hero has to involuntarily expose the secret places in his life that he has tried to conceal. It is in these places that leaders tremble with fear, weary about looking like a failure in the eyes of those who are the mirror that reflects an image of everything they claim to be. Because of their deceitfulness and unwillingness to be honest with themselves, they look for a credible rationale, desiring comfort in an uncomfortable situation, to justify their reasons for escaping. The most commonly used excuse they give to try and make right the wrong they have committed is that the mirror they looked into reflected back to them the image of a man they never knew was there. Their inability to recognize the individual they act like when they are wounded and in sin causes them to place the responsibility for this individual on someone or something else besides themselves. In this case, that something would have to be the faultiness of the mirror, the excuse they use to justify why they could not connect with the image it reflects.

There are three kinds of mirrors that reflect back to us images of how God sees us, of how we see ourselves, and of how we are seen in the eyes of those around us. Like a photographer that goes through the necessary process to develop a photo, each mirror is placed strategically, in sequential order to verify the authenticity of the image it reflects. This process is explained more clearly in Matthew 22:

> *You shall love the Lord your God with all your heart, with all your soul and with your entire mind. This is the first and great commandment. And the second is like it: You shall love your neighbor as yourself* (Matthew 22:37-39, NKJV).

The first of the three mirrors that we encounter is called the "Word." From the very beginning of time, God's desire for mankind was for us, through His Word to render a perfect reflection of His love. Scripture declares that God is love. So, when God looks down at humanity through the mirror of His Word, He expects His love, working through us, to be the reflection He sees starring back at Him. God's greatest purpose for humanity is for us to reflect a perfect image of Him making it virtually impossible for anyone to distinguish between the two of us. We can do this by loving God with all our heart, soul, mind, and strength. God will never allow us to out love Him. For God, loving us is not enough. He has and will always out love us. It is not until we begin loving God with all that we have that we are able to see how much greater His love is for us than even the love we claim to have for ourselves. It is at this point that we should embrace His love and begin to love ourselves with the unconditional love He loves us with. The honesty of this reflection is then based on God's Word:

> *The Word of God is living and active. Sharper than any double edge sword, it penetrates to dividing soul and spirit, joints and morrow; it judges the thoughts and intents of the heart. Nothing in all creation is hidden from God's sight. Everything is uncovered and laid bare before the eyes of Him to whom we must give an account* (Hebrews 4:12, NIV).

The Word of God gives us an accurate reading on the extended depths God is willing to go to reveal the sincerity of His love toward us. The word mirror then reflects for us the transparency of true love and its ability to break through the bloody wounds and countless failures of our fragile countenance.

Because of our regained consciousness of His love towards us, we provide our neighbors with opportunities to recognize true love and what it really looks like in the eyes of an invisible God whose presence can only be reflected through our love. For this reflection, we have to look into the mirror called "YOU." Scripture says that God desires for us to love our neighbor the same way we love ourselves. So how do you love YOU? Now that we know God's love for us is greater than the love we claim to have for ourselves, we need to learn how to love ourselves with His unconditional love. God's love, when understood, is so amazing that we often times are overwhelmed by it. His love for us is so great that even if we were to try and keep it to ourselves we could not because it is too much for any one person to contain. So this second mirror captures for us an image of God working on a masterpiece that reflects the infinite depths His love is willing to travel to restore us back into an original. This leads us to the last mirror called "The Neighbor."

In order for the infinite depths of God's unconditional love to be understood, its objective, the person to which it is directed, will always challenge the channel it flows through to verify it as a direct link to the original source from which it says it originates. The channel is us and it is at this junction in the developmental process that we are able to closely examine the extended depths we are willing to go to show our unconditional love for God. The objective here is our neighbor. Our neighbors are the mirrors around us that show us how to love others out of those pits where we ourselves were once trapped. The various degrees of love we claim to have for God are always measured by how much we love our neighbor. It is impossible for us to love God whom we cannot see and not love our neighbor whom we see every day. When we love our neighbors with His unconditional love, then we can honestly say that we know how to love ourselves unconditionally. This mirror then reflects the image of unconditional love that has been tested and has proven its ability to last under any condition.

Each of the three mirrors spoken of here has been strategically placed in sequential order to recapture the authenticity of an image that we were previously acquainted with. Because of our prior exposure with the perfected image we desire to reflect, our minds have been programmed to recognize imitations and identify counterfeits. These mirrors therefore remind us of the godly image in which we were created and call for us to live a life that agrees with its demands. In our imperfect world, the reflection of the image and the private life of the individual fail to embrace their oneness, because of the failure of one to acknowledge and validate the existence of the other.

The one-sided perspective of the superhero, unchecked by the fragilely framed physique of a wounded soldier, causes leaders to chase after a distorted perception of the God image in which they were created. Now because of their unwillingness to expose those hidden places of vulnerability, once and possibly still present in their lives, they carve out an idol image of themselves that allows them to escape the demands of the God image they no longer feel they are qualified to reflect.

When a distorted perception of the God image becomes deeply embedded in their psyche, it promises them the pleasure of a never ending orgasm, never accomplished through relations with their spouse, but only through those acts of worship they perform unto themselves in an attempt to satisfy their selfish ambitions. The idol, therefore, is a damaged copy that tries to excuse itself from the historical background of the original image, claiming victory without honoring the wounded soldier whose shoulders it had to stand on to successfully achieve his purpose. Now it appears that the skillfully carved out image, shaped after ideas formed through a bad reception in the limited realm of our imagination, tries to rejoice over its attempted assassination of the wounded personality it hopes to remove from the history of his story. Convinced that he has been removed, like an evil villain omitted out of the pages of a thriller, the idol image is caught off guard when he begins to see the confusion of his story without the strengthening testimony of his wounded past. He then comes to conclude that the height of his success can only be measured from the deep depths of the wounded places from where he had to recover.

The valley lows we see in a superhero's journey remind us of God's power to work through the frailties of our weak and feeble flesh. Most people fail to realize that the true hero in the saga is not the superhero, but it is his oftentimes overlooked partner in crime, his alter ego. Some may question the validity of this statement, but believe me it is true. Superman would have never been able to rescue and save so many lives without the sensitive ears and eyes of Mr. Kent. Likewise, a superhero's ability to dwell among the people enables him to experience the people's needs first hand. Because of his close connection with humanity's strengths and weaknesses, his inner hero is able to meet the needs of people with a supernatural force rooted and grounded in love. He is able to empathize with the condition of those he was assigned to help, because he was subjected to those same temptations that expose God's power in us to the evils of our society. The book of Hebrews, Chapter 4, verses 15-16, had this to say about the greatest leader of all time, Jesus our Great High Priest: *For we do not have a high priest who is unable to sympathize with our weaknesses, but we have one who has been tempted in every way, just as we are—yet was without sin* (Hebrews 4:15-16, NIV).

It is impossible to appreciate the strength of the superhero and his story without first looking back into the history of the weak and feeble man he most often likes to forget about. Likewise it is impossible to understand the mission and the mandate of Jesus, without first examining the degrees of separation that existed between God and humanity as a consequence of Adam's fall. Many leaders try to appreciate the joys of victory without first learning how to appreciate the pains of defeat. Adam's fall was necessary in order for humanity to understand love's ability to exist far beyond humanity's badly bruised, scarred, and mentally unstable conditions. The possibility of defeat always calls for us to question whether or not we can continue to be what we were created to be, even when it appears that defeat is inevitable. Jesus is the expressed image of God's love, the Mediator, standing ready to articulate, for both God and mankind, the strengthening power that makes the two of them inseparable. The strengthening power referred to here is called "LOVE." Scripture says it like this through the eyes of the apostle Paul:

> *For I am convinced that neither death nor life, neither angels nor demons, neither the present nor the future, nor powers, neither height or depth, nor anything else in all creation, will be able to separate us form the love of God that is in Christ Jesus our Lord* (Romans 8:38-39, NIV).

According to Scripture, God is love. The verb *is,* in English is a third person singular verb in the present tense. Third person is the person you are speaking about within the context of a conversation you are having with another person. In other words the author acknowledging that he is highlights to others his understanding of God's immutability. God still is and continues to exist as what He has always been, love. Leaders must understand that what God said they are is still what God expects them to be no matter what present conditions they may face. The great heights to which the superhero was able to soar would have been unattainable without the empathetic posture towards the silences of his alter ego. The greatest strength through which these two became one inseparable force is the only resolution to a conflict that sometimes makes the two contemplate divorce. The celebrity life of the superhero without the history of his alter ego is nothing more than the beautiful greenery we notice around what on the outside appears to be a mansion lavished with the finer things in life. Upon further analysis it is discovered that the decorative exterior of the home was added only to hide the badly rotted siding and wood that supports its foundation. Because of years of neglect and the lack of upkeep, the value of the mansion has slowly depreciated far below its intended value.

The superhero is the beautiful greenery that we love to look at with eyes full of admiration. He is the decorative exterior of the mansion that captures our attention and intrigues us to turn and look in amazement. But without the upkeep of his alter ego, the foundation of the superhero will crumble and his value will continue to slowly depreciate over time.

So I ask you today, have you neglected and underestimated the testimony of your alter ego? What role, if any, has he played in your superhero's saga? Honestly, when you look in the mirror do you really see in you what God said about you? Do you?

Chapter Four

Oh No, He Didn't!
The Eulogy Written by the Sexy
and Vivacious Ms. Destiny

"Lady of My Life," a 70's hit song, written by Mr. Man in the Mirror himself, Michael Jackson, is one of the most beautifully composed songs ever written. Michael helped me as well as men all over the world to articulate our love for that one woman God destined to be the Lady of our Lives. This song became the national anthem for men in love with that special lady with whom God intended for them to enjoy the rest of their lives. At one point in the song suddenly out of nowhere, Michael filled with the joy of a man mesmerized by the inner beauty of the woman that ignites his fire and desire shouts as one overwhelmed, searching for the words to explain the beauty he has been blessed to behold. At a loss for words, he exhales with a joy unspeakable and an excitement that cannot be contained.

This is the masculine groaning of a man in love who is unable to fully articulate in words that loving feeling. With a down beat and a shout of "**Whoooo**," Michael captivated listeners with his ability to articulate with a groan the love that he once attempted to articulate with his words. *"Lady of My Life"* provided men of all ages and ethnicities with a one-way pass on to the love boat, granting every man the opportunity to rediscover his unconditional love for the one woman with whom God had previously acquainted him. Yes, the intimacy the two previously shared enables them to reconnect with the previous pattern of movement traveled by a God that predestined for the two of them to be together. Now, Michael's lady echoes back to her love those valuable words every man needs to hear, affirming him as her soulmate and singing for him her response to his expression of love:

> *"If, only you knew,*
> *How much I do*
> *Do love you."*

Like any novice, full of zealous aspirations, ready to conqueror those inevitable challenges that await the arrival of the two inexperienced lovers in a world they have never explored, the ecstasy with which both the pursuer and the pursued are adamantly convinced will last forever creates a false sense of entitlement in the eyes of the women we claim we love. The fantasy, or the unrealistic expectations that can only be achieved in a perfect world, becomes the heavily weighted rubric the ladies of our lives use to measure the distance between the night and shining armor we pretended to be when we first met and the angry, bitter, and selfish man we promised them we never were or ever could become.

The damaging residue that still remains from previous relationships and the premature exposure to those men God never equipped with whatever it was our lady loves needed at the time have caused us to deny the existence of the untamed animal most of us still are, hoping to live up to the demands our women believe their fantasy entitles them to. Like a woman scorned, fearful, and afraid that she will never find in her love the perfection she once looked to find in her father, the fickle imagination of the broken hearted sets out on a journey to find the world's idling image of a man that is nonexistent. The idea of the superhero now arises to the forefront of every woman's psyche, assuming that destiny expels the possibility of their mate's insufficiency. The legacy of the fictional macho man character, therefore, becomes the mirroring reflection of the man to whom every man will constantly be compared.

In our effort to walk in the shoes of the fictitious character our ladies have scripted for us to portray in their fantasy, we neglect the wisdom of God for our lives that sees us in the capacity for which He created us, never expecting us to be anything more or less than what He said we should be. As men, in our desire to distance ourselves from the imposturous images that have distorted the imagination of the women we love, we attempt to act like their savior, riding in to their lives on a donkey while they cry out in a loud voice "Hosanna." The conflict between the image of the man she fantasizes about and the godly image in which we were created to be becomes the turning point of this very familiar love triangle. The dilemma over whether or not to reveal the substance of the packaging through which the unrealistic image is reflected ignites within us the desire to excommunicate all of the fraudulent activity from our mack daddy portfolios, replacing the history of a wound past with the highlights of what we hope will be a promising future.

The internal conflict between the two dueling personalities calls for us to measure the deep depths to which our love is willing to extend itself, declaring that the product we have advertised is God's best deal and a worthy enough investment for the women we were destined to love to submit their lives to. The love affair between the superhero lover and his beloved damsel in distress is now abruptly disrupted by the emergence of the clumsy, unattractive, and vulnerable side of her love, his alter ego. From the contagious love that brought the two of them together to the secret identity of her hero that might cause them to forever be apart, the energy with which Ms. Destiny and her superhero are drawn to one another causes those of us intrigued by this relationship to further investigate the passions that would ultimately cause these two opposites to attract.

Whooooo! The jaw dropping beauty of the sexy and vivacious Ms. Destiny is the epitome of a masterpiece, skillfully crafted in a time past, capturing the thoughts of the first man, Adam, as he stood drooling over the anatomy of his comparable suitor, Eve. Finally, the long and anticipated arrival of the one and only woman blessed with the kind of beauty capable of making a grown man echo the words of one of the greatest rap songs of all times, *"I Need Love,"* has arrived. Yes, in the words of the once beloved internationally known Rhythm and Blues group, Dru Hill, "Beau-ty is Her Name!" As she invades the thoughts of the supposedly impenetrable steel that guards the mind of her **Hercules, Hercules,** she releases into his atmosphere a sweet smelling aroma that cause his eyes to open as he waits anxiously to see an appearance of the inevitable beauty that must accompany her fragrance. As she enters into the many compartments of his mind, she moves with elegance other women admire and a sexiness that stimulates him not only sexually, but intellectually as well.

Aroused first by the excellence of her spirit, he now enters into a deeper dimension of intimacy that brings a satisfying pleasure to the two of them in the absence of all sexual contact. Crippled by the favor that violently pursues after the innocence of her heart, her destined lover cautiously attempts to get her to recognize that the love she once knew is the same love reflecting for her the purpose for which God saw the need to release her from and then to reintroduce her to this destiny that ultimately inspired her creation. Like Adam, the superhero has now risen from his deep sleep awakened by the presence of the only help sufficient enough to draw him away from looking for love in all the wrong places. In the book of Genesis the search for an objective someone like him to whom he can extend his love introduces for the first time in Scripture God's heavily integrated theme of reconciliation:

> *So the man gave names to all the livestock, the birds of the air and all the beast of the field. But for Adam no suitable helper **was found**. So the Lord God caused the man to fall into a deep sleep; and while he was sleeping, He took one of the man's ribs and closed up the place with flesh. **Then the Lord God made a woman from the rib He had taken out of the man, and He (God) brought her to the man.** The man said, "This is now bone of my bones and flesh of my flesh; she shall be called Woman, for she was taken out of Man." For this reason a man will leave his father and mother and be united with his wife, **and they will become one flesh*** (Genesis 2:20-24, NIV).

The echoing theme of the two, Adam and Eve, becoming one introduces God's intentions through Scripture to attract two objectives, once joined together before, to recapture that loving feeling with that special one God had previously acquainted them with in the beginning. The reunion between the once separated duo confirms the reality of Adam's longing for the tangible presence of the partner only God could bring back to his remembrance. Eve then is a gift from God, given and used as one of His primary forces of energy, created with the power to either motivate Adam towards or discourage him away from becoming the man God ultimately desired for him to become. Like Eve, the superheroes' Ms. Destiny is also the gift that God has given to them, the superheroes of this generation. Not only does their sexiness cause them to have an erection, but their love for God causes them to stand at attention before their heavenly Commander-in-Chief. Now graced with the privilege of dwelling in her presence, the depths of their love for God can be more accurately assessed by Ms. Destiny, showing them the consistency between the authenticity of their confessions and the motivations of their hearts. Ms. Destiny in the life of the superhero is that good thing he is searching to find and the favor of God he needs to become the hero God desires him to be. Unfortunately the imagination of Ms. Destiny has been corrupted by her distorted perception of the superhero that she saw in her fantasy and the imperfections that lie within the superhero. Though these two images appear to be conflicting, the man she thought he was and the man he really is are not that different.

As the superhero and his love, Ms. Destiny, commit themselves to the joys and disappointment that will follow them as they set out on their romantic journey, the love that they have confessed is now challenged by external forces that call into question the motives of the heart with which they said they believe. For every verbal commitment the superhero made and for every vow he promised to keep, the reality of the person he declared he was is now challenged by those evil habits of the person he forgot to tell Ms. Destiny all about. As they close the ecstasy dimension of their relationship and enter into a dimension called reality, Ms. Destiny is surprisingly forced to examine whether or not the declaration she made to the superhero when she first reconnected with his love will continued to be honored by the faithful desires of her heart which he has now broken. Stunned, standing in disbelief, she wonders, "How could I not have seen or known of his struggle?"

Ms. Destiny now stands face-to-face with his once silent alter ego, not sure if she is ready to hear about the pains, wounds, failures, and addictions that not only existed in his past, but exists in his present also. As she listens to the unfamiliar voice of the man she never knew, crying profusely, waiting for the voice of the man she is in love with to denounce these unruly allegations brought up against him, she expels from her thinking the fantasy of the unrealistic image of the flawless macho man she was looking for in her reality. To her surprise after expelling from her thinking the distorted perception of the man she thought he was supposed to be, she had to confront the reality of the weaknesses she saw in him before they became one and how she was willing to deny the existence of his blemishes, hoping to guarantee the reality of the man that could only exist in her fantasy. Continuing to search for an escape from the madness that now causes her to question if whether or not she would have given her superhero the time of day if made aware of his insufficiencies at the beginning of their romantic journey, her decision to move forward becomes halted by the unconditional love that now tightly grips and holds her heart captive. Under the weighted pressure of God's love, her heart conforms to God's perfect will, causing her to surrender herself to the only one she desires and to the only one God desired for her to have.

Now revived, awakened from the fantasy that once plagued her reality, she cries out from her secret place that this is no ordinary love. No longer blinded by the potential of what she thought he could become, she commits her heart only to him, challenging him to be the God man God expects him to be. Clearly she is the epitome of what godly love truly is. As love moves and allows her pursuer to chase after her, the violent cries of those she once had given the VIP treatment in the privacy of her inner circle rise up against her, furiously yelling chants of "Kill the liar! He is the devil." Ms. Destiny cries out, "Is it a crime that I still want you?"

As the case against Ms. Destiny and the superhero begins, her prosecutors attempt to destroy the credibility of what God joined together and what they say the two of them were stupid enough to believe. Like Eve facing the wisdom and craftiness of the serpent, Ms. Destiny presents her case, intent on convincing her accusers that God said the two of them were meant to be together. As the evil jurors deliberate over the unlawful evidence presented at her trial, they are overwhelm-ingly surprised by the oneness that accompanies Ms. Destiny and her pursuer when they walk in the room. Still confronted by the evidence that proves these two should not even be in the same room let alone together, the jurors proceed to render a verdict according to the prosecution's system of law: "In the case of *Ms. Destiny, I'm in Love with a Superhero, File #111,* we the jury find the defendant guilty and have determined that the de-fendant and her lover have no justifiable reasons for being together." The judge sentences her to a bitterly painful and unhappy future should she continue to de-light in the company of this supposed imposter.

While her critics boast in what they believe was a sure victory that will convince her to concede to their wishes, to their amazement she continues to live her life by every word that proceeds out of the mouth of God who brought them together. Distinguishing herself from the gullible woman at the beginning of Genesis Chapter 3, Ms. Destiny refuses to respond to any of the questions of her critics, allowing God through her relationship with the superhero to come to His own defense. Outraged by her peaceful posture which far supersedes their limited comprehension, the lead prosecutor declares to the appreciation of the lis-tening audience that Ms. Destiny's wounded pursuer is not the right one for her and that she should look for another. Drooling like a pack of ravaging hounds anx-iously waiting for the chance to engage in on their prey, the audience waits quietly, determining that there is no response she can give to justify her love for the superhero's alter ego. Standing to her feet, supported only by God and the man she has vowed to love, she quiets her emotions, listening to hear, and ready to speak out loudly God's affirmation of the only man He has anointed with the strength to love her. As she stands, overwhelmed with a mixture of emotions, she zealously speaks a declaration to those questioning what kind of love is this. With one deep breath she exhales revealing the intentions of her heart through the window of this poetic dissertation:

"Shattered dreams of an image I perceived to be more real than my realist reality, I was once choked by a fantasy that tricked me into holding on to the nonexistent idea of a man God still has yet to and never will create. With my vision obscured by a false sense of entitlement that caused me to lust after an ideal man God said would never satisfy me, I flirted with many hoping to catch the one who could stimulate my body, mind, and soul. After measuring each possibility to a standard of unrealistic expectations, I surrendered my desires to the will of the one sitting higher than I. Through the power of my submission to God, the manifestation of the superhero God anointed with the resources to love me the way I needed to be loved reconnected me with the perfect idea of the woman I was created to be in Eve.

Like Adam, dumbfounded after awakening from his deep sleep, blessed only to behold the radiance of the woman God fashioned in his likeness, I now arise from a place of dormancy to boldly announce to some and to declare to others the death of the man in my fantasy I thought God anointed me to love. Yes, the idea of the man my doubt caused me to fantasize about is deceased and his image erased from emotions once stimulated by the pleasure of his adulterous touch. With his legacy expelled from the desires of my heart, his absence in death liberated me to carefully examine my readiness for God to present me as an offering to his afflicted reflection. Like the widowed Moabitess Ruth, I too have gleaned unknowingly in the field of my Boaz. I was honored with the opportunity to witness his evolution from the pains of his wounded past to his transformation into the king God created him to be.

As the lady of his life, I therefore count it a privilege to eulogize my fantasy and accept the testimony of his alter ego, the packaging that bears up under the weight of the superhero all of you, his accusers, have denied him the right be. Yes, to you, his ruthlessly relentless accusers, it is with great pleasure that I present to you the evolution of a superhero in this my eulogy entitled "Oh No He Didn't" written by me, the sexy and vivacious Ms. Destiny, the only woman God anointed with the strength to love my man the way he needs to be loved.

Chapter Five

Mind Over Matter:
The Mastermind behind the Diabolical Schemes of the Ruthless, Relentless Accuser of the Brethren

As the innocence of the master's original idea searches for a womb fertile enough to conceive its substance, the diabolical schemes of wickedness are employed to abort the reality of an authentic thought. The abundantly fertile substance through which the seed desires to breakthrough will explain the formation of an idea others hope to perceive correctly. Like the horrific cry of a lost soul pleading for the restoration of its innocence, the once silent voice of evil spills out the lethargic slurs of hopelessness, encouraging the vessel empowered to carry God's image to disqualify itself from this privilege.

The never-ending dual in the mind of the superhero intensifies as the Creator seeks to reveal the intentions of an authentic idea fused into the embedded psyche of the sacrifice he has chosen to give expression to his thought. The sacrifice, in this case, the hero, though created as an earthen channel intended to reflect the energy with which all things are sustained, is unfortunately confronted with the persecution of an arch nemesis who continues to search unsuccessfully on how to distinguish between the presenter and the originator of the idea. In his quest to denounce the authenticity shared between God and the mirror that reveals his expression, the accuser of the brethren seeks, through whatever accessible door he is allowed to walk through, to invade the varying dimensions of God's power, destroying the expression of his image through the ignorance of the unlearned.

Hosea 4:6 reads, *"My people are destroyed from lack of knowledge."* The lack of knowledge referred to here is due largely in part to the behavior of the unruly priests dwelling in the Northern Kingdom of Israel. Israel's ignorance of its power is clearly a reflection on the ignorance of its spiritual advisors, the priests. Here we see the priests teaching what they thought they knew, but were unable to produce, in themselves, what they caused their followers to believe they were. So now the people were left to hold on to a form of power, but remain ignorant and unlearned with regard to the depths of God's power working in them. As a result, the arch nemesis relentlessly seeks after an opportunity to consume the people through the ignorance of the priests with the temptations of life, desiring to destroy them with their own power, power that they are too immature and unskilled to practically apply.

If knowledge is power, then the ignorance of the unlearned will cause the superhero to relinquish his power into the hands of an enemy that will counter attack with tactical maneuvers created to cause submission through the over exertion of energy or force the hero uses to defend himself. In other words, the power we fail to control is the power we freely give to our enemy to kill us. Unlike Adam who relinquished the power of all humanity over to the serpent, or Samson who revealed the origin of his strength to a sexy Philistine woman named Delilah, who assisted the Philistines in his capture, the superhero can defeat his accuser by denouncing his strength and putting on the conquering strength of the only contender immune to the wicked plans of our accuser, Jesus Christ.

The conquering strength of Jesus Christ working in the favor of the superhero is undoubtedly the only source of quantitative energy sufficient enough to qualify the hero to become the godly leader his nemesis tries to convince him he could never be. Jesus, better referred to in the Hebrew as "Yeshua," is according to Scripture the epitome of everything God, in the beginning, called for humanity to be in order to reflect an authentic expression that would validate his existence in the realm of human consciousness. In the beginning of time, God created man in his image, and man, not by constraint but by choice, fell to the seductively aggressive schemes of his enemy, distorting his perception of the image in which he was created. From that time on, man had sought and searched after an exact representation of God's person that would model for all an expression on how to practically apply God's power in an effort to cripple those daily proclivities exuding through the walls of his fleshly pores. After thousands of years searching for a solution that would relieve mankind from the pain of its battle wounds, God provided humanity with a remedy filled with more than enough power to ensure the continuity of the man's health and eternal existence. God's remedy is called "Yeshua" who is the Christ.

According to Philippians 2:5-8, *"Your attitude should be the same as that of Christ Jesus: Who, being in the very nature of God did not consider equality with God something to be grasped, but made Himself nothing, **taking the very nature of a servant**, being made in the **human likeness**. And **being found in appearance as a man** humbled Himself even to the death of the cross"* (Philippians 2:5-8, NIV). Scriptures also reveals that when Jesus prayed He asked the Father to glorify Him with the glory He had once before: *"I have brought You glory on the earth by completing the work You gave Me to do. And now, Father, glorify Me in Your presence **with the glory I had with You before the world**"* (St. John 17:4, NIV).

The question then arises: With what glory did Jesus perform His miracles, signs and wonders if He is requesting for the Father to glorify Him with the glory *He had* before the world was? It is clear that Philippians 2 reveals the package through which Jesus used to give expression to God's power residing in the fleshy pores of the human anatomy. Jesus did not dethrone Himself, descend down through forty and two generation, and land on earth with the same glory the angels honored Him with in heaven.

Jesus' purpose for coming to earth was never to show us God's glory working in Him, but for Him to model an example of God's glory working in us. The Scripture says that He made Himself nothing, even though He was an equal with God. He took on the form of a servant, being made in human likeness, and being found in the appearance as a man. In other words, He became us. Jesus took off His glory because the weight of it was too heavy for us to bear up under. So He, instead, picked up and put on the falling glory of humanity that was lost by Adam in the Garden of Eden, dwelt among men, and proceeded to model for us all how to use the glory God originally blessed mankind with in the beginning to overcome the wiles of his enemy. When Jesus walked the earth, healing the sick, raising the dead, and casting out demons, He did that clothed in our glory. Possessed by the power of the Holy Spirit, Jesus performed for us what the apostle Paul in Romans 7:18 says he was unable to discover how to perform within himself. Wow!

Once leaders can attest to the reality of Jesus in this light, not diminishing the reality of His human condition as it relates to theirs, they then can assert the conquering strength of their Redeemer working in them to weaken the diabolical schemes of their relentlessly ruthless accuser. Once the true identity of the villain, attempting to disqualify them from their destiny is revealed and the ignorance of the unlearned is replaced with the intelligence of the Holy Spirit, the superhero will be strengthened with might, ready to conquer the challenges posed by both his external and internal enemies.

To every leader, expected to live up to the heroic feats that accompany the fame of the superhero, remember never to deny your listening audience the right to conclude the reality of who you are without the testimony of your alter ego. Be honest with yourself so that you can help to liberate those assigned to your anointing. Never be afraid to confront the man starring back at you when you look in the mirror, even when he does not look like what God said he should be. Remember, the greatest enemy existing in your present reality is you. So unmask the true identity of your inner hero. The world is anxiously waiting and demanding for you to be the hero God anointed you to be.

Until the next book, be blessed.

Contact Information

To inquire about Pastor Shaun Saunders speaking, ministering, or doing book signing and discussions at your event, you may contact him by writing to:

Pastor Shaun Saunders
100 North Creek Trail
Jonesboro, GA 30238

You may also send him an email at:

thewoundedleader12@gmail.com

Connect with him on Twitter at:

www.twitter.com/ShaunSaunders3

CPSIA information can be obtained at www.ICGtesting.com
Printed in the USA
LVOW132018200313

325287LV00001B/4/P